THE RODIN
MUSEUM OF
PARIS

Portrait of Rodin   by John Sargent   (1856-1925)
Antechamber for the Duchess of Maine's Officers, Salon 4

THE RODIN MUSEUM OF PARIS

Photography
NICOLAI CANETTI

Introduction
MONIQUE LAURENT Curator, Rodin Museum

Commentary
SANDY LESBERG

PEEBLES PRESS
New York · London

154600

First Published 1977 by
Peebles Press International, Inc.
10 Columbus Circle, New York, New York 10019

DESIGNED BY NICOLAI CANETTI

© 1977 Peebles Press International, Inc.
ISBN 0-672-52364-7
ISBN 0-672-52370-1 Collectors' Limited Edition
Library of Congress Catalog Card Number 77-75351

Acknowledgements
We acknowledge with great gratitude the cooperation of
M. Jean Chatelain. Administrator of the Musée Rodin of Paris.

Distributed by
The Bobbs-Merrill Co., Inc.
4300 West 62nd St., Indianapolis, Indiana 46268, U.S.A.
in the United States and Canada

Barrie & Jenkins
24 Highbury Crescent
London N5 1RX, England
in the U.K., Ireland, New Zealand and South Africa

Printed and bound in the United States of America

The Rodin Museum is a magical place. Filled with artwork of vital importance, bedecked with roses, embellished by lawns and foliage, it offers visitors a haven beyond the reach of time, a peaceful setting whose deep, muted colors encourage quiet pleasure, happiness and dreams.

How did this artistocratic dwelling, known as the Hôtel Biron, escape demolition and the demeaning alterations that doomed or defaced so many historic buildings? Why, for some sixty years, has it housed Rodin's sculptures, work which was central to the birth of modern art and which has nourished most of the major artistic trends of this century? These are the questions we will examine here.

Our story begins in the late 17th century. Before that time, the western boundaries of Paris barely encompassed the Louvre and the Tuilerie Gardens and except for the Abbey of Saint-Germain des Près, there was little construction on the Left Bank of the Seine. But this situation was rapidly chainging. In 1670, Louis XIV had built the noble Hôtel des Invalides on a flat expanse of land bordering the river in an area called Grenelle. Les Invalides was designed to house wounded war veterans and soldiers grown too old for battle. The presence of this splendid, royally endowed establishment quickly drew attention to a heretofore uninhabited section of the Left Bank, and *grands seigneurs* fleeing a stifling, overcrowded Paris began settling in what was already known as the Faubourg Saint-Germain, where the low price of land permitted residents to plant large gardens and enhance their properties with convenient outbuildings. Upon Louis XIV's death in 1715, the Court left Versailles, reinstating Paris as the true French capital. With the rise of the sophisticated *salons,* some literary, others financially oriented, and the emergence of a powerful new class grown rich through speculation, the fashionable Faubourg was soon dotted with sumptuous private dwellings. The Hôtel Biron was among them.

Despite its grandiose name, the handsome mansion had humble origins. It was built by a nouveau riche hairdresser, Abraham Peyrenc, who came to Paris as a youth to seek his fortune. After a modest start as a manservant-barber, Peyrenc's lot quickly improved. His quick wits and skillful exploitation of a chance to cause a scandal, allowed him to marry the daughter of his wealthy, bourgeois employer. He had conveniently seduced the girl. Thanks to the financial climate and his participation in Scotsman John Law's system of paper currency, Peyrenc amassed a fortune: the purchase of a property called de Moras earned him a title.

After serving first as counselor then steward to the Duchess of Bourbon, Peyrenc decided in 1727 that his dazzling riches deserved a worthy setting and he ordered "the most superb house Paris had ever seen" to be built on the rue de Varenne. The plans were drawn up by Jacques Gabriel, Inspector-General of Royal Buildings, and the construction was done under the supervision of Jean Aubert, architect of the Main Stables at the Château de Chantilly. In 1731,

Abraham Peyrenc de Moras and his family moved into their mansion whose floor plan measured more than 43 meters long by 20 meters wide. A handsome courtyard occupying over 1500 square meters stretched before the dwelling and the stables, located in the angle formed by the rue de Varenne and the boulevard des Invalides, the site today of a gallery devoted to special exhibits, were large enough to house thirty-three horses.

Alas, the former barber died in 1732. His widow surrendered her sumptuous home to the Duchess of Maine, granddaughter of Louis II de Condé (known as the Grand Condé) and daughter-in-law of Louis XIV through her marriage to one of the king's legitimized bastard sons borne by the royal favorite, the Marquise of Montespan. Enamored of intrigue, wealth and pleasure, the Duchess of Maine had been leading a glamorous, frivolous life surrounded by a court of her own which she had established at her handsome château in Sceaux. But her participation in a conspiracy aimed at undermining the power of the Regent, Philip of Orleans, after Louis XIV's death, her subsequent imprisonment and the death of her husband after a terrible illness, darkened her later years. Still, a circle of faithful friends remained loyal to the end, among them Voltaire, who dedicated several works to the Duchess and wrote the short story *Zadig* at her home.

The Duchess of Maine spent sixteen years in the house on the rue de Varenne, dying there in 1753 at the age of seventy-seven of "complications from a cold she couldn't shake off." During her residency, she made numerous improvements. To the left of the main courtyard she had a three-story building constructed in which to lodge her steward, equerries, chaplain, secretary and physicians (it has since disappeared). To the courtyard's left, in what today is a garden containing *Le Penseur* (*The Thinker*), the Duchess installed a series of outbuildings around a farmyard, adding kitchens, servants' halls and carriage houses to Peyrenc de Moras' stables. Finally, she had the side of the house facing the gardens decorated with carved wood as well as providing for various interior alterations.

Upon the Duchess' death, the mansion passed into the hands of the Duke and Duchess of Biron, who gave it the name it would henceforth bear. The Duke had won his laurels as Field Marshal de Gontaut-Biron fighting for Louis XV. In 1745, during the Battle of Fontenoy, in which Field Marshal de Saxe defeated the Anglo-Austrian forces, de Biron had five horses wounded or killed beneath him.

Inspired by his love for the ostentatious, Field Marshal de Biron transformed the Duchess' slightly dowdy residence into an elegant showplace and sophisticated meeting spot. In his *Memoirs,* the Duke de Croy recalls: "Overnight (the Hôtel Biron) became a gathering place of the highest refinement, where guests enjoyed themselves thoroughly . . . The Field Marshal's open table, laid for thirty, was popular among beautiful women of all nations." One of the Duke's receptions has gone down in history, a party given in 1782 by a regiment of the

French Guards in which de Biron held the rank of colonel quartered near the mansion. The occasion was the visit of the Grand Duke of Russia, the future Tsar Paul I, and his wife, who were touring Western Europe as the Count and Countess du Nord. Needless to say, their disguise fooled no one.

The Duke de Biron appears to have loved his gardens above all else. They were open to the public as was the custom with many aristocratic and noble properties, including Versailles. Thus visitors to the rue de Varenne could gape at the floral arrangements—particularly a famous tulip garden—the elegantly clipped greenery, the shrubs, the trellised porticos, the grottos and the Chinese pavilions constructed by the Duke to enliven his symmetrical garden *à la Francaise* with elements stemming from a new vogue for the casual "English garden," closer to "nature's way." (During this same period, Queen Marie Antoinette was ordering similar changes made in the gardens of her Trianon Palace.) The Duke de Biron was also responsible for the creation of a decorative basin on the property. And it is said that the first nectarines to be seen in the French capital were grown on his grounds. His truck garden, orchards, fig trees and melons were considered "one of the wonders of Paris."

Upon the aged Field Marshal's death, the mansion passed into the hands of his nephew and godson, the Duke de Lauzun. Dashing and adventuresome, the Duke served in turn as an officer in Louis XIV's army, a comrade-in-arms of La Fayette and de Rochambeau during the American Revolution, and a general in the French National Convention, holding commands in the Revolutionary Army of the Rhine (1792) and participating in the War of Vendée (1793) against Royalist forces. Despite his efforts for the Revolutionary cause, de Lauzun was suspected of half-heartedness and expired on the scaffold at the end of 1793.

After the Duke's demise, the Hôtel Biron was inherited by the Charost-Bethune family, who lived there peacefully throughout the Revolutionary era. During this time of turmoil, the mansion escaped damage of any kind, undoubtedly thanks to the Duke de Charost's reputation as the public-spirited founder of several philanthropic institutions.

The stress and horror of the Reign of Terror gradually abated under the Directoire, leaving Paris plunged into a feverish whirl of activity as a privileged society headily savored the disappearance of the Committee of Public Welfare and an end to the killing. The de Charost family profited from the general air of excitement by leasing the Hôtel's grounds to professional organizers of public entertainment, who scheduled dances, games, fireworks and acrobatic and juggling acts on the property. In fact, the Hôtel Biron was the site, in 1797, of the first attempt to parachute jump from a balloon, which unfortunately ripped before leaving the ground, much to the crowd's dismay. Needless to say, the transformation of the property into an amusement center wrought havoc with its beautifully tended gardens.

The reign of Napoleon I marked the end of the mansion's splendors, which fell victim to the times. Cardinal Caprara, a Papal Legate who, as Archbishop of Milan, had anointed Napoleon King of Italy, occupied the Hôtel from 1806 to 1808. It was then converted by Prince Kourakine into Russia's diplomatic headquarters in Paris. But its stint as the Russian Embassy was short-lived, thanks to Napoleon's declaration of war on Tsar Alexander in 1812.

With the Russian's departure, the Duchess de Charost lived alone in her mansion until 1820. A pious woman, she wanted her home to be used for godly purposes after her death and thus sold it for a minimal sum to a religious community known as the *Dames du Sacré-Coeur,* a group reminiscent of the *Compagnie de Jesus* founded in 1804 and devoted to the education of young women. Mother Sophie Barat, leader of the congregation, focused her impressive energies on creating a boarding school designed to welcome girls from the upper aristocracy and even royal princesses. The high level of instruction and the worldliness of the student body earned the school a dazzling reputation, attracting among others Mademoiselle Della Rovere, a descendant of Pope Julius II, and Eugenie de Montijo, who as wife of Napoleon III went on to reign as Empress of France. In 1830, one hundred and fifty students, fifty novices and twenty-five postulants occupied the mansion and the resulting cramped quarters forced the *Dames du Sacré-Coeur* to build dormitories, dining halls and various other annexes around the courtyard, as well as to utilize the existing outbuildings. In 1875-1876, the boarding school was completed with the addition of a neo-gothic chapel, designed by the renowned architect Gustave Lisch. Located to the right of the main entrance and built on the site originally used for the stables, the chapel serves today as a gallery for special exhibits.

In the early years of the twentieth century, France's Third Republic was rocked by a grave political and religious crisis, which ended with the severing of diplomatic relations with the Vatican and the separation of the Church and State in 1905. These developments precipitated the suppression of religious groups and the *Sacré-Coeur* boarding school was forced to close its doors. In 1907, while waiting for the mansion's demolition and replacement by a rental apartment building, a trustee divided up the Hôtel into several small lodgings. This turned out to be the mansion's salvation, since the hastily created units quickly attracted artists drawn by the beautiful surroundings. Among them were the poet Jean Cocteau, the painter Henri Matisse, the dancer Isadora Duncan and most important of all, that master of written German, Rainer Maria Rilke, who had earlier served as Rodin's secretary and now encouraged the sculptor to rent several rooms in the Hôtel as a storage place for his work and his extensive and varied collection *of objets d'art.* This collection—which belongs today to the Rodin Museum as we shall shortly see—ranged from Egyptian, Greek and Roman pieces through carvings executed during the Middle Ages, from rare Japanese prints through nineteenth century "chinoiserie," as well as including such masterpieces as Van Gogh's *Portrait of Father Tanguy,* which Rodin purchased on the advice of his playwright-friend Octave Mirbeau, and Renoir's *Nude,* obtained for 25,000 francs shortly after 1900 from the famous dealer Ambroise Vollard.

During the years 1908-1909, Rodin reached the height of his fame. After a particularly painful start, during which he was forced to work for fellow sculptors to stay alive, he managed through sheer determination, when approaching forty, to gain acceptance for his conception of a form of sculpture free of academic strictures and oriented towards the study of man. His striking creative gift, founded on a thorough understanding of classical art and the workings of nature, transcended the conventions of his times, ultimately winning over art lovers and critics. The important Paris Exposition of 1900 assured his success by including the first major retrospective of his work. This gave his reputation the boost it needed, enabling him to expand his studio space in order to handle the commissions flowing in from an international clientele, a significant number of whom were American. His American-born friend the Duchess of Choiseul, the dancer Lois Fuller and the illustrious photographer Edward Steichen helped introduce his work to the United States and elsewhere throughout the world.

Thus it was a man of worldwide renown who daily left his home—the Villa des Brillants in suburban Meudon—for the handsome Paris mansion where he joyfully worked and happily welcomed his friends, revelling in the enchantment of the gardens run wild.

Spurred on by a press campaign waged by journalist Gustave Coquiot in two leading dailies, *Le Figaro* and *Le Journal,* a plan to create a museum to serve as a showplace for Rodin's assembled work began to take form. His strong newspaper backing gave Rodin the leverage necessary to plead with his influential friends in government to halt plans to raze the Hôtel Biron. Rodin's efforts eventually bore fruit and two years later, in 1911, the French Government purchased both grounds and buildings, allocating them to the Ministry of Public Information and Beaux-Arts without specifying how the property would be used. It was at this point that Judith Cladel, daughter of Rodin's friend the journalist Leon Cladel, herself a newspaperwoman, critic and Rodin's biographer, redoubled her efforts to build up a wave of public opinion reinforced by political backing and artists' petitions which would promote the conversion of the Hôtel Biron into a "Rodin Museum." But the government was considering other proposals as well, among them a plan to turn the Hôtel into an administrative building or a palace destined to welcome foreign officials visiting the French capital. In order to gain approval for the projected museum, Rodin would have to overcome the hostility he had engendered in certain influential circles as well as combatting governmental reluctance to cede property to a living artist, no matter how renowned.

Finally, in 1914, the constant pressure exerted by Rodin's friends on such political figures as Paul Boncourt, Raymond Poincaré, Marcel Sembat and Georges Clémenceau resulted in the introduction of draft legislation creating a Rodin Museum. But due to the onset of World War I and its terrible aftermath, the issue was not resolved until 1916. During the intervening years, Rodin, despite his fragile health, struggled to coordinate arrangements for the final disposition of his work. His efforts bore fruit in the form of three formal notarial deeds dated April 1, September 13 and October 25, 1916 by which Rodin unconditionally donated his complete art collection, correspondence, written work, documents, archives, property in Meudon and above all his entire artistic output—both sculpture and drawings—to the French government as well as all reproduction rights to the above. Reserving for himself only a modest sum deriving from the reproduction of his bronzes during his lifetime, he literally made the French government his heir. In return, the state, after impassioned debates, accepted his donation with the Law of December 22, 1916 and created the Rodin Museum in the Hôtel Biron. In accordance with the artist's wishes, the Hôtel became a national museum managed by a Board of Directors and guaranteed financial autonomy by special statute. This very real autonomy has remained possible thanks to monies accruing from control of the reproduction rights to all of the master's works, the French legislature having appointed the Museum sole heir to Rodin's artistic output until 1982.

In 1919, the Hôtel Biron-Rodin Museum opened its lofty portals to the public. It has not closed them ever since.

To enter the historic dwelling, the visitor must cross the courtyard whose worn paving stones bear witness to the Duchess of Maine's horses and carriages. To the right, the first monumental casting of *Le Penseur* (*The Thinker*) is silhouetted against the imposing dome of the neighboring Invalides. Nearby, Balzac's massive frame looms beneath the tall trees. To the left stands the *Porte de l'Enfer* (*The Gates of Hell*), cast in 1937, whose writhing hordes suffer the torments of the damned, under the watchful eyes of the *Bourgeois de Calais* (*The Burghers of Calais*) "like a rosary of pain" to quote the artist.

Bordering the courtyard stands the Hôtel: a long, severe facade fashioned of white stone, whose starkness is relieved by the delicate tracery of its wrought iron balconies and the masks carved into the window stones, said to be stylized portraits of the Peyrenc de Moras family.

The facade overlooking the garden is more richly appointed, with a wide wrought iron balcony supported by elaborately curved stone brackets in a typically rococo style and a large, triangular pediment carving believed to represent the Duchess of Maine as an allegorical Mother crowned by Glory. From the spacious terrace which gives onto the grounds, the visitor can descend into the garden restored around 1930 in a style reminiscent of the 18th century. Some of Rodin's most beautiful bronzes stand on this part of the grounds: the *Cariatide à l'urne* (*The Caryatid Before the Urn*), the *Cariatide à la pierre* (*The Stone Caryatid*), *Meditation*, the *Grande Ombre* (*The Large Shadow*) and *Eve*. At one end of the lawn, the round, stone-edged basin, filled in by the nuns of *Sacré-Coeur* to provide a base for a statue of the Virgin Mary, has been restored to its original form. Its center is graced by a bronze enlargement of one of the most dramatic elements of the *Porte de l'Enfer, Ugolin et ses Enfants* (*Ugolin and His Children*).

Entering the museum, the visitor finds sixteen rooms which house the body of Rodin's sculptures, pieces dating from his youth, showing the influence of the 18th century and Carpeaux through the audacious *Mouvements de Dance* (*Dance Motions*) executed in his final years. Studies for monuments, busts, and bronze and marble group pieces are scattered through the Museum along with a profusion of drawings and watercolors which Rodin produced throughout his lifetime, in a continual creative outpouring. The arrangement of the work seems at times contradictory: a chronological approach occasionally gives way to groupings by theme, which in turn are subject to factors imposed by the Hôtel's age and aesthetic imperatives.

Indeed, the mansion still conserves some of its initial decor. Originally the Hôtel was appointed with *boiseries* in the purest rococo style, carved wooden panels embellished with intricately carved seashells, leaves and rosettes painted white and gold. Tall mirrors, marble chimney pieces and pediments framed paintings depicting scenes from mythology; cornices were graced with bas-reliefs portraying the Fables of La Fontaine, and wrought iron railings and exquisite furnishings completed an ensemble which each of the Hôtel's 18th century owners took joy in enriching.

Alas, the transformation of the mansion into a religious boarding school in the 19th century had disastrous results. The zealous *Dames du Sacré-Coeur*, unwilling to expose their students to any but pious and edifying sights, sold every decorative element which struck them as frivolous.

Patient restoration has resulted in the complete or partial re-creation of the original decor. Traces of past splendor can be seen in the white and black marble pavings, the mosaic parquets, the handsome stone medallion which graces the main staircase. Several years ago, four of the ground floor rooms facing the garden were fitted out with their original carved wood panelling, which had luckily been unearthed. Although the *boiseries* have lost their white and gold covering, this matchless panelling remains one of the most beautiful decorative ensembles of the first half of the 18th century to be found in Paris today. And its presence makes it easier to visualize the original uses to which these stately reception rooms were put in the days of the Duchess of Maine. Moving from east to west they were known as follows: the Great East Room, which presently houses the *Age d'airain* (*The Bronze Age*); the Common Room or Antechamber for the Duchess' Officers, which now contains the *Eternelle Idole* (*The Eternal Idol*); the Central Salon, featuring *Le Baiser* (*The Kiss*), the scene of dazzling receptions; the Assembly Room or Duchess' Parade Room, now the Camille Claudel room, and the Great West Room. The original dining room was situated in what today serves as the reception hall and souvenir counter, while the second floor chambers were devoted to lodging the mistress of the house's ladies-in-waiting.

The Rodin Museum unites two elements vital to the history of western art. First among them is the Hôtel Biron, an almost perfect specimen of Regency architecture and decor, whose harmonious proportions and rational dimensions give it a human scale rather than the overwhelming proportions that dwarf and discourage visitors to so many famous palaces. Although the museum's rooms are spacious, they are not cavernous and one senses that the Hôtel could have served as a dwelling as well as exhibition space for a sophisticated public.

The second element is Rodin himself. An independent spirit, Rodin sums up and dominates sculpture at the end of the 19th century while simultaneously preparing the way for new modes of expression.

Often he is portrayed as a rebel reacting against his time. In reality, he was closely connected with the artists of the Middle Age and of the Renaissance, and beyond that, with Rome and ancient Greece, through his research, personal taste and artistic training. Rodin used the human body to personalize passion in the traditional sense; he does not seem to have had sympathetic relations with those artists who, at the beginning of the 20th century, experimented with other means of expressing the human condition.

Yet Rodin broke with the artists of his time in his refusal to follow any rule of pre-established construction, thus his horror of the Academy, which he felt deadened inspiration by enclosing it in a repertoire of mimicry of gestures and attitudes defined in advance. On the contrary, Rodin is "modern" in the sense that he gave priority to intuition, sensibility and sensation which he put in the service of an uncommon creative power.

His life, entirely dominated by his vocation as sculptor, confuses itself with his work.

Born in a very modest milieu, he was forced to earn his living at an early age, and it is above all as an artisan working for ornamental painters and decorators that he trained himself in the practice of sculpture and acquired a technical virtuosity that surprised his contemporaries.

His first personal works, such as the *Mask of the Man with a Broken Nose* (1864), transmit a powerful naturalism. In 1875, while traveling in Italy, Rodin found new inspiration in the sculpture of the Italian Renaissance, particularly that of Michelangelo. *The Age of Bronze* (1876), the first large detailed study of a live model done upon his return, is marked by this influence. When completed, the quality of his modeling seemed so surprisingly real that Rodin was accused of having cast from life.

Further progress is shown in the *Walking Man* and *St. John the Baptist* (1878) as Rodin steadily gained in expressive power.

In 1880, Rodin received the commission for a monumental door in bronze destined for an official building. The result was the famous *The Gates of Hell,* never unveiled during Rodin's lifetime. The torments and unsatisfied aspirations of the human soul are found in the tangled forms, connected one to another by the movements and attitudes rendered with an audacious freedom of concept and execution. A good number of the figures of *The Gates of Hell* were treated individually by Rodin and have become famous: *The Thinker, The Prodigal Son, She Who Was Once the Helmet-Maker's Beautiful Wife,* etc.

The monument to the Burghers of Calais, for which Rodin was commissioned in 1884, was planned in a complex fashion. This group of six persons illustrating an episode occuring between France and England during the Hundred Years' War was preceded by numerous studies. Similarly, Balzac commissioned in 1892 by the Société des Gens de Lettres, was the object of a multitude of sketches and projects evoking each physical or psychological aspect of the novelist. The result, a surprisingly varied collection, was finally realized in a single, large simplified form, without doubt one of the most thrilling and most striking created by the artist.

One ought not to neglect Rodin's activity as a portraitist of the society of his time, especially since after 1900, his international fame attracted both a large and diverse group of individuals who wished to model for him. In all these personages—aristocrats, artists, or friends—an untiring appetite for human nature allowed him to translate the model honestly, without ever sinking to mean detail.

Similarly, in a powerfully free technique, he expressed himself in thousands of drawings and watercolors, frequently dominated by his obsession for the female form.

The half-century which has elapsed since the death of Rodin has seen the world shaken by multiple tragedies and by many close escapes from brutal events. However, it is striking to realize that the significance of his work has resisted all these trials and that in his contribution lives the incarnation of a creative force.

His body of work is so extensive that it is difficult to confine it within a school or style as one tends to do with other artists for simplicity's sake. In reality, as both a summing up of 19th century art and one of its dominating forces, Rodin's sculpture is at once passionately and lyrically romantic, realistic thanks to the artist's close ties with nature, and symbolic, according greater weight to a gesture's significance than to its verisimilitude. Combining synthesis with innovation, Rodin's *oeuvre* marks the birth of modern art.

The Hôtel Biron's measured elegance coupled with the creative power of the work it houses make the Rodin Museum one of the most poetic sites in Paris. The photographs which follow render its incomparable atmosphere with great sensitivity.

—Monique Laurent

1. *Northwest facade of the Hôtel Biron bordered by the Courtyard of Honor*
The Thinker Bronze 1880 in the foreground

2. *The Burghers of Calais* Bronze 1884-1895
Rue de Varenne in the background.   The front garden of the Rodin Museum

In 1342, during the Hundred Years' War, six men from Calais
gave themselves up to King Edward III of England during an
eleven-month siege of their city. The exchange was the result of an
arrangement between Calais and England—six citizens would
sacrifice their lives if Edward would put an end to the siege.
Froissart describes the men as ". . . bare-headed, barefooted, with
ropes around their necks and having in their hands the keys of the
town, trudging up the path to the suffering and death they nobly
accepted." They were eventually released when the Queen took pity
on them and pleaded with her husband on their behalf.

3. *The Gates of Hell* Bronze 1880-1917
Cast in the garden of the Rodin Museum in 1938

"I used to think that movement was the chief thing in sculpture and in all I did, it was what I tried to attain. My *Gates of Hell* are the record of these strivings . . . There I have made movement yield all it can." — A. Rodin

Yet it was not only movement that Rodin tried to achieve in this work — *The Gates of Hell* portrays Rodin's expression of the deep human suffering that results when passion overcomes reason. *The Gates* was originally intended for the Museum of Decorative Arts, although it was never used and was not cast until after Rodin's death. The style of the doors reflects the influence of Gothic, Renaissance and Baroque church architecture on Rodin. He referred to *The Gates* as his "Noah's Ark," and for over thirty-seven years he used *The Gates of Hell* to experiment with his theories about the human body and about architecture. Some of Rodin's most famous sculptures stem from his work on *The Gates — The Thinker, The Kiss, Fugitive Love, The Prodigal Son, She Who Was Once the Helmet-Maker's Beautiful Wife, Ugolino, Adam, Eve, The Three Shades.* Over one hundred eighty-seven figures were included in the final version of *The Gates*, but the individual figures and groups that comprise *The Gates of Hell* are physically as well as morally isolated, for he obviously felt that the torments of damnation must be borne alone.

4. *The Three Shades* Plaster 1880
Crowning group on *The Gates of Hell*. A bronze cast stands on the first landing of the Stairway of Honor

The figures, direct descendants of the art of Michelangelo, represent the futility of resistance to the pull of Death.

5. *The Gates of Hell*   Framed by the figures of *Adam* 1880 and *Eve* '1881.
The garden of the Rodin Museum

6. *Adam* Bronze 1880
Standing near *The Gates of Hell* in the garden of the Rodin Museum

Adam is also an offspring of *The Gates of Hell*. Rodin first
modeled, and later destroyed, a figure of Adam in 1875 when he
returned from Rome, where he had been inspired by the works of
Michelangelo. The resemblance to Michelangelo's *The Slave* is
striking even in this later piece. Rodin used as his model an athlete
from the fairgrounds who displayed a very real strength that was
remarkably latent and subdued. Perhaps the athlete's stance evoked
in Rodin the feeling of Adam's rude awakening from the Garden of
Eden—a man who has not yet begun to realize his power.

7. *The Martyr*   Bronze   1885   Landing on the Stairway of Honor

The Martyr was originally a standing figure in Rodin's work *The
Gates of Hell*. Seen in the context of *The Gates, The Martyr* portrays
the agony of a lost soul—one who, governed by uncontrolled passion,
sacrifices his most precious possession—his life. Yet there is a daring
quality in the way Rodin exhibits the recumbent figure, starkly,
without any base or pedestal.

8. *The Martyr* Landing on the Stairway of Honor

9.   *The Reverend Father Eymard*   Bronze   1863
Superior of the Fathers of the Very Holy Sacrament   Salon 1

Rodin joined the religious order—the Fathers of the Very Holy
Sacrament—in 1862 when his sister died. Father Eymard, who
realized Rodin's true calling, encouraged him to devote himself
to his sculpture.

10. *Young Woman with Flowers in Her Hat*   Terra-cotta   1865-1870   Salon 1

The model for this bust was Rose Beuret, "the little seamstress" as she was called, who shared with Rodin over fifty years of his life. They were finally married when Rose was sixty-eight years old, eighteen days before she died.

11. *Young Woman with Flowers in Her Hat*   Salon 1

12. *Young Mother* Bronze 1885 Salon 2

Rose Beuret posed with Rodin's son Auguste-Eugene Rodin for this sculpture. Shortly after Rodin completed the piece, the boy fell, injuring his head, and as a result remained emotionally disturbed throughout his life.

JEUNE MÈRE

13. *Young Mother in the Grotto* Plaster 1885 Salon 2

In this work, Rodin links the image of a grotto to that of motherhood. The effect exalts, almost sanctifies motherhood—in that the grotto can be seen as a natural protective retreat, like a womb as well as a holy shrine. That Rodin does not refer to the sculpture's possible religious implication—for the image of mother and child evokes that of Mary and Jesus—can be seen as expressing his oft-stated feeling that there is no difference between the Virgin Mary and any other mother, since all life is equally sacred.

14. Overview of the Great East Room Salon 3
Bust of Jean Dalou Bronze 1883 and *The Age of Bronze* Bronze 1875-1876
in the foreground on the left

15. *Young Girl Listening*   Plaster   1878
Great East Room, Salon 3

"I often begin with one intention and finish with another. While
fashioning my clay, I see in fancy something that has been lying
dormant in my memory and which rises up before me in what seems
to be a vision created by myself. I know it is not this, but a suggested
combination of form which I must have already perceived in nature,
and which has never before aroused in me the image that
corresponds to it. And then as I go on, and the execution becomes
more complete, there is a sort of reverse process in my mind, and
that which I have made reacts on my perception of nature, and I
find resemblances and fresh analogies which fill me with joy." —A. Rodin

16. *The Age of Bronze* 1875-1876
Great East Room, Salon 3

In 1871, Rodin left Paris for Brussels, where he found a model,
Auguste Neyte, a young Belgian soldier, who posed for him for
eighteen months. *The Age of Bronze* was the result of Rodin's work.
When shown at the Cercle Artistique in Brussels in January, 1877, it
aroused keen interest. "One of our talented sculptors, Mr. Rodin . . .
exhibits a statue which is to be shown at the coming Paris
Exhibition," wrote one critic. "It will certainly not go unnoticed for
it attracts attention by its strangeness; it holds it by a quality as
precious as it is rare—life. This is not the place to discuss how far
there was casting from life." In Paris reviewers asserted similar
accusations.

"I remember they said (my *Age of Bronze*) was cast from life . . . I
was shocked at the injustice, the infamy of it . . . I
protest(ed) and demand(ed) justice of so odiously unfair a judgment.
(It was) suggested I have a moulding made of my model and
let them compare. The model agreed. I sent mouldings and
photographs to the Salon: the box was never opened."—A. Rodin

17. *The Age of Bronze* Salon 3

18. *Eugene Guillaume* Bronze 1903
Great East Room, Salon 3

Eugene Guillaume was a member of the Beaux-Arts and the
Academie Française, who, at first, criticized Rodin's sculpture but
later admired his work.

"In working on a bust, or in fact on any figure, I always carefully
model by profiles, not from a merely front view. I give depth and
solidarity, volume . . . and location in space. I do this however with a
line that starts from one's own brain. I mean that I note the
deviation of the head from the face. In another, the lower jaw bulges
out in contrast with the receding forehead. With this line of
deviation established, I unite all the profiles and thus get the
life-like form." — A. Rodin

19. *Madame Alfred Roll* Marble 1884
Great East Room, Salon 3

Mme. Roll was the wife of Rodin's friend, M. Alfred Roll, who was a rather successful painter of society portraits.

20. *Madame Alfred Roll*   Salon 3

21. *Call to Arms* Bronze 1879 Great East Room, Salon 3

In 1878, Rodin unsuccessfully tried to obtain the commission for a monument to commemorate the Franco-Prussian War of 1870. The work, *Call to Arms,* was inspired by François Rude's *La Marseillaise.* In Rodin's sculpture, however, the warrior is wounded, a reference to the human vulnerability of Rodin's heroes. The desperate figure of France, for which Rose Beuret posed, rallies the dying soldier.

22.   *Call to Arms*   The garden in the background.   Salon 3

23. *Bust of Lady Sackville-West* Marble 1914
Great East Room, Salon 3

"The artist, in representing the universe as he imagines it, formulates
his own dreams. In nature, he celebrates his own soul. And so he
enriches the soul of humanity. For in coloring the material world
with his spirit he reveals to his delighted fellow beings a thousand
unsuspected shades of feeling . . . He gives them new reason for
loving life, new inner lights to guide them." — A. Rodin

24. *Aurora and Tithon* Marble before 1906
Great East Room, Salon 3

___

"Great artists proceed as Nature composes, not as anatomy
describes. They do not carve a particular muscle or nerve or
bone for its own sake. They see and express the whole and by
broad planes, their work throbs with light or sinks into shade . . .
The expression of life, to preserve the infinite suppleness of reality,
must never be frozen and fixed." — A. Rodin

Rodin portrayed in this work the moment in classical mythology
when Aurora, goddess of the dawn, agonizes over the loss of her
mortal love, Tithon, for whom she asked the gods to grant
immortality. She neglected, however, to ask for eternal youth, and
unable to stand the decrepitude that age had incurred upon her
lover, Aurora allowed him to leave the earth for the Land of
the Shades.

25.   Overview of the Antechamber for the Duchess of Maine's Officers, Salon 4
First Funerary Spirits   Stone   1900   in the center
Eternal Idol   Plaster with patina   1889   in the mirror

26. *First Funerary Spirits* Stone 1900
Antechamber for the Duchess of Maine's Officers, Salon 4

Originally intended for a monument to Rodin's friend, the mural painter Puvis de Chavannes, the diaphanous figures seem to melt one into another in a trance-like ritual of death. Their unfocused gaze evokes the vaporous quality of spirits, which conflicts with their solidly rendered limbs. Rodin contrasts the physical presence with the spiritual absence of a corpse.

28. *Eternal Idol*   Plaster with patina   1889
Wooden panels, rendered in the style of Rocaille. Antechamber for the Duchess of Maine's Officers, Salon 4

"One dares not give it meaning. It has a thousand meanings," wrote Rainer Maria Rilke, who was at one point Rodin's secretary. The piece was originally created for *The Gates of Hell*.

29. *Eternal Idol*   Salon 4

30. *Adam and Eve* Marble 1884
Antechamber for the Duchess of Maine's Officers, Salon 4

Rodin used subjects from classical and Biblical sources because he saw in them an expression of his view of love as playful and uninhibited and essentially physical.

"Love is essentially copulation, the rest is only detail, doubtless charming, but detail nevertheless." — A. Rodin

31. *Madame Rodin* Marble 1898
Antechamber for the Duchess of Maine's Officers, Salon 4

Rodin expresses his profound reverence for woman in this portrait
of Rose Beuret, later to become Madame Rodin, by evoking in her
face a quality of inner strength while losing none of its femininity.

"In portraits of (men) . . . we must pierce without pity the innermost
crannies of their souls, must strip them of disguise, lay bare the
intemperate, even vicious passions that surge in them daily . . . But a
portrait of a woman is another thing, their nature is not ours, we are
far from grasping it; we must therefore be respectful and discreet.
We must be circumspect in unveiling their tender and delicate
mystery. Even with them, always the truth, but not always all the
truth. Sometimes we may, just a little, drop the veil. —A. Rodin

32. *Eternal Spring* Bronze 1884
Antechamber for the Duchess of Maine's Officers, Salon 4

Eternal Spring was among the first works in the cycle of romantic sculpture which includes Rodin's well-known piece *The Kiss*.

Rodin exhibited the statue in the Salon des Artistes Français in 1898 under the title *Cupid and Psyche*; it has also been called *Zephyr and Earth*. A beautiful young woman, Adele, with whom he worked frequently over a four-year period, posed for the work. *Torso of Adele* (1882) was a pivotal piece for Rodin, since he used the form with its graceful blending contours for many of his later works.

33.   Overview of the Great Central Salon, Salon 5
From left to right: *Saint John the Baptist*   Bronze   1878; *Torso of a Young
Woman*   Bronze   1909; *The Cathedral*   Stone   1908; *The Hand of God*
Marble   1898; *The Secret*   Marble   1910; *Flying Bronze*   Bronze   1890-1891;
The Kiss   Marble   1886; *Woman — half figure*   Bronze   1910

34. *The Cathedral* Stone 1908 Great Central Salon, Salon 5

The Cathedral evokes the spiritual purpose of its title in the figure of
two hands joined loosely together as if in prayer, as well as suggesting
the shape of the vault intrinsic to Gothic architecture. While it is not
at first apparent, the hands are those of two people who face one
another, perhaps suggesting human interrelationship as being
essential to achieving the spiritual ideal.

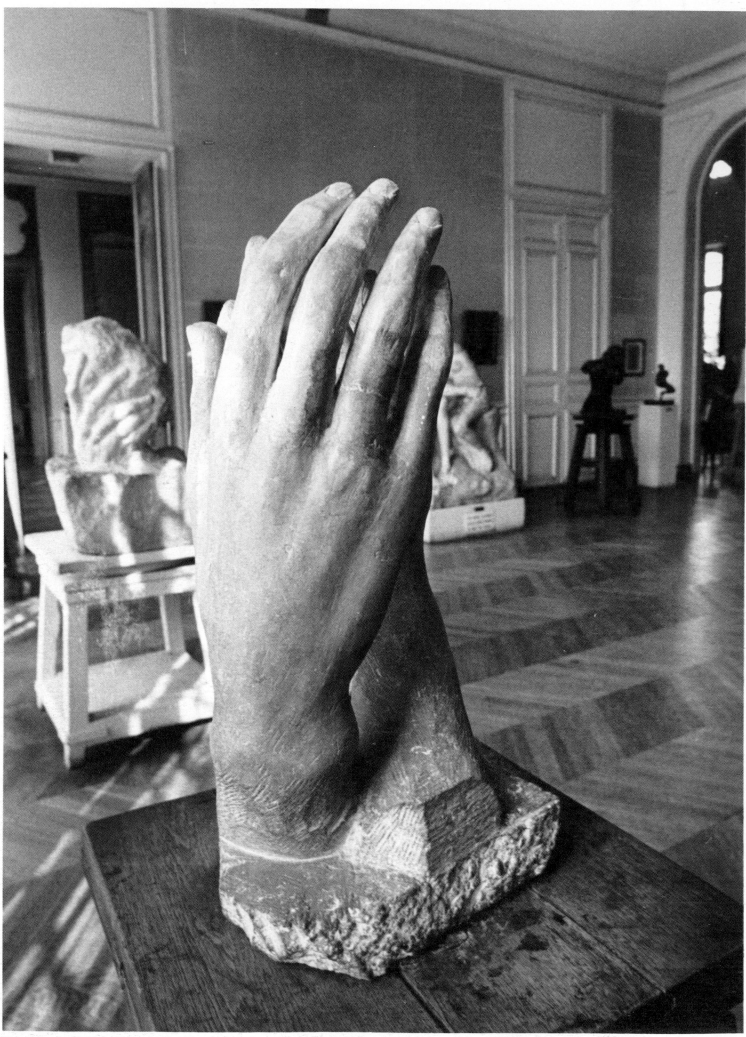

35. *The Cathedral* Salon 5

36. *The Cathedral* Salon 5

37. *The Cathedral*   Long view of the garden in the background. Salon 5

38. Overview of the Great Salon, Salon 5
The Cathedral Stone 1908 in the foreground
The Hand of God Marble 1898
and *The Kiss* Marble 1886 in the background

39. *The Prayer* Bronze 1909
Iris, Messenger of the Gods Bronze 1890-1891 and *Walking Man* Bronze
1877-78 in the background. Great Central Salon, Salon 5

"Never consider a surface as any thing but the extremity of a
volume . . . Instead of imagining the parts of a body as more or
less flat surfaces, I represented them as projections of interior
volumes. I endeavored to express every swelling of torso and limbs,
the efflorescence of a muscle or bone extending deep under the skin.
And so the truth of my figures, instead of being superficial, seems to
blossom forth from within like life itself." — A. Rodin

40. *The Hand of God*   Marble   1898   Great Central Salon, Salon 5

The unconventional representation of the process of creation in
Rodin's work *The Hand of God* aroused public criticism, particularly
focused on his use of rough marble in the completed piece. Rodin
often left uncut stone around his sculpture, thus capturing the
birth and unfolding of form.

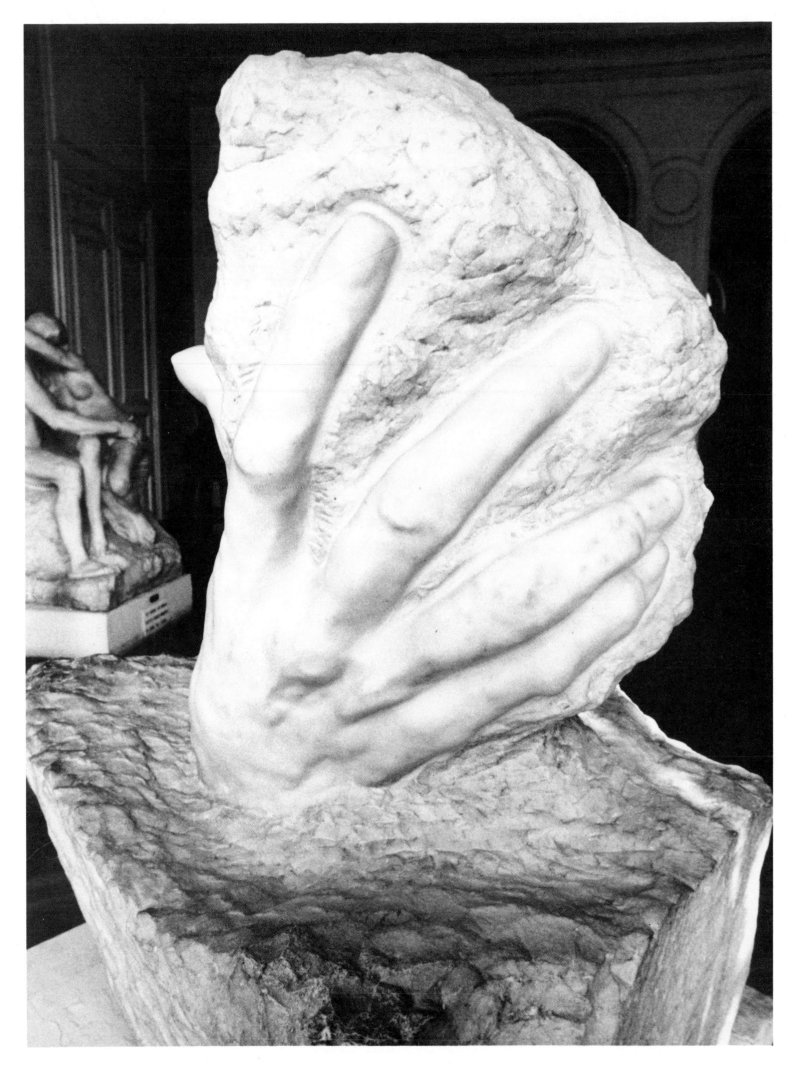

41. *The Hand of God* Salon 5

42. *The Hand of God* Salon 5

43. *The Kiss*   Marble   1886   Great Central Salon, Salon 5

Originally rendered for *The Gates of Hell*, its basic concept was to portray lust conquering reason. It has since been transformed into a universal symbol of romantic liaison even though Rodin's original concept is evident by observing the tension that is created by the detached beauty of cold marble contrasting with the warmth of human passion.

In 1893 to avoid public outrage, the organizers of the Chicago Exhibition placed *The Kiss* in a private room and admitted only those with a special card.

THE VISITORS ARE REMINDED
THAT IT IS STRICTLY PROHIBITED
STATUES

44. *The Kiss* Salon 5

45. *The Kiss* Salon 5

46. *The Kiss* Salon 5

47. *The Kiss* Salon 5

48. *Flying Figure* Bronze 1890-1891
The Kiss Marble 1886 in the background. On the walls, several paintings by
Eugene Carriere (1849-1906), a friend of Rodin. Great Central Salon, Salon 5

This sculpture illustrates Rodin's ability to integrate a truncated
limb into the contour of the work while cutting it at right angles to
the vertical axis. The idea of exhibiting a piece with limbs bluntly
severed shocked his neo-classic predecessors, who rendered all forms
in their complete state. Thus Rodin creates a tension between the
vitality of the bodies depicted in his work and the fact that
these bodies are not living but are, rather, works of art. This
tension points to the art of the sculptor, and is emphasized by the
lack of balance intrinsic to the placement of the limbs.

49. *The Secret* Marble 1910 Great Central Salon, Salon 5

". . . All the best work of any artist must be bathed in
mystery . . . That is why many of my figures have a hand, a foot
still imprisoned in the marble block; life is everywhere, but rarely
indeed does it come to complete expression . . ." — A. Rodin

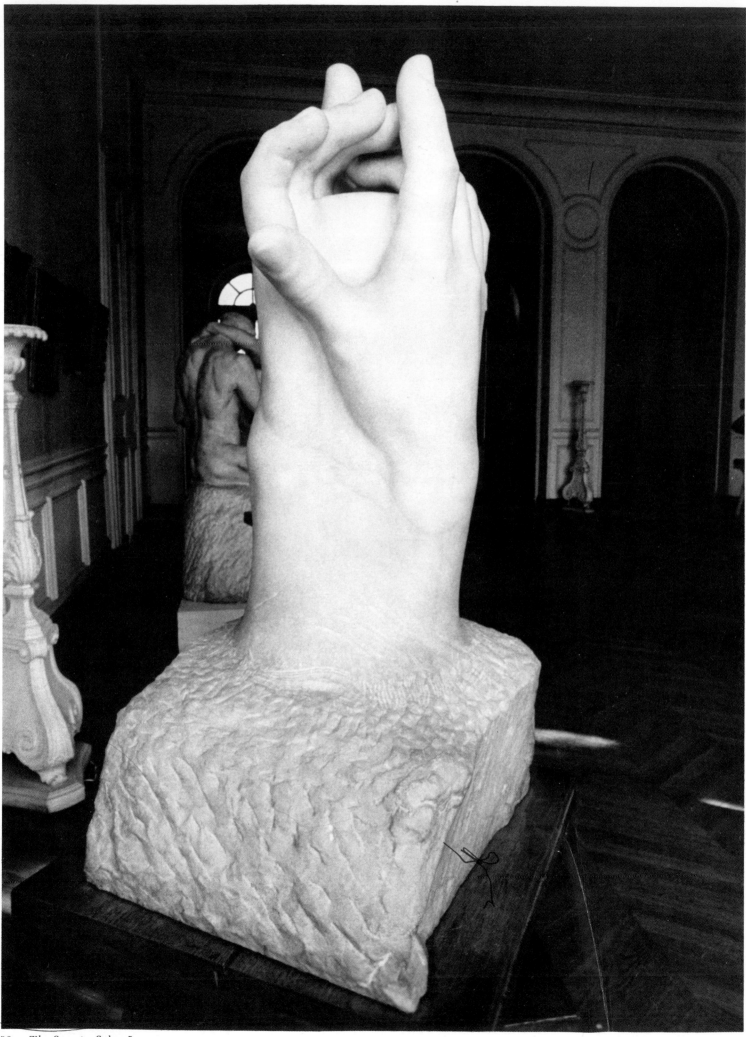

50. *The Secret* Salon 5

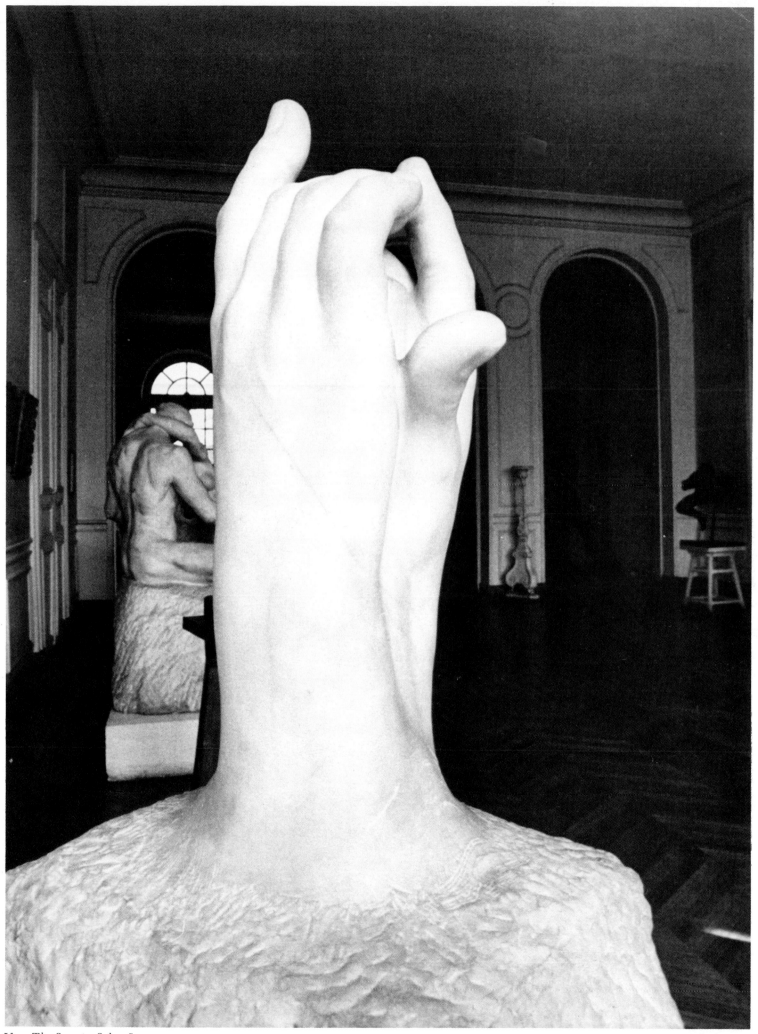

51. *The Secret* Salon 5

52. *Saint John the Baptist* Bronze 1878
The Prayer Bronze 1909 In the background. On the wall, a copy of
Rembrandt's *Bathsheba* by Ricard. Great Central Salon, Salon 5

Rodin used a robust Italian peasant, Pignatelli, for his model, who
had never posed before; Rodin told him to hold his head up, talk
continually and use his arms in animated gestures while walking.
The statue of John the Baptist evokes the feeling of a man walking,
although Rodin placed both feet of the statue on the ground.

"I have always tried to render inner feeling by the mobility of
muscles. In . . . art the illusion of life can only be obtained by good
modelling and by movement. These are the blood and breath of all
great works." — A. Rodin

53. Overview of the Duchess of Maine's Parade Room, Salon 6
Orpheus Bronze 1892 in the center
Around the salon, several works by Camille Claudel (1864-1943), sculptress,
friend of and collaborator with Rodin, as well as several works by Rodin, for
which Camille Claudel served as his model.

54. *Orpheus*   Bronze   1892   Duchess of Maine's Parade Room, Salon 6

"I accentuate the lines which best express the spiritual state that I
interpret . . . I accentuate the muscles which express distress . . . I
have exaggerated the straining of the tendons which indicate the
outburst of prayer." — A. Rodin

55. *Orpheus* Salon 6

56. *Thought*   Marble   1886-1889   Duchess of Maine's Parade Room, Salon 6

Rodin used Camille Claudel, the talented sculptress who was his
pupil and mistress for fifteen years, as the model for this work. She
eventually went mad, and spent the last thirty years of her life in
an institution. Her younger brother, Paul Claudel, who was a
well-known dramatist, offered an explanation for her madness:
consistent with her intense spirit, when she realized that she could
never totally possess Rodin, she gave up and lost her senses. She was
twenty-two when she posed for *Thought* and Rodin was forty-six.
Despite her youth, Rodin was able to perceive her determination
and rare intelligence, which he captured in the sculpture.

58. *France* Bronze 1905
Duchess of Maine's Parade Room, Salon 6

Camille Claudel, the ill-fated pupil and mistress of Rodin, posed
for this allegorical bust, which has also been called *Byzantine
Princess* and *Empress of the Lower Nile*. All names suggest a proud,
strong woman whose influence on the development of civilization is
unwavering because it is primordial and eternal. In 1912, the
French government gave Crown Point, New York, a cast of the
work to commemorate the three hundredth anniversary of Lake
Champlain.

59. *Eve* Bronze 1881 Great West Room, Salon 7

Here is the complete woman. She is nude yet she covers her
face with modesty. Her body lines are graceful and round, yet her
sturdy lower limbs indicate a feeling of mother earth. She is at
once vulnerable and giving, while appearing to retreat into her own
small circle of existence.

The beautiful Italian woman who served as Rodin's model for *Eve*
was in fact pregnant, although he was unaware of this while working
on the statue. The complex figure of *Eve* that finally emerged
satisfied Rodin and he allowed the statue to stand, even though he
fired the model after she had told him of her condition.

60.   Overview of the Great West Room, Salon 7
Eve   Bronze   1881   in the center
Centauress   Marble   1889   on the left

61. *Eve* Salon 7

64.   Overview of the Great West Room, Salon 7
Eve   Bronze   1881   on the left
The Wave   Marble   before 1887   on the right

65. *Siren—Meditation* Stone 1885
Great West Room, Salon 7

"In a human body, the contour is given by the place where the body ends, thus it is the body which makes the shape. I place the model so that the light, outlining it against a background, illuminates the contour . . . I change positions and that of my model, thus I see another contour . . . Since the human body has an infinite number of contours, I multiply them as far as possible." — A. Rodin

66. *Siren—Toilette of Venus* Stone about 1884
Great West Room, Salon 7

"A woman undressing, how dazzling. It's like the sun piercing through the clouds." — A. Rodin

67. *The Wave*   Marble   before 1887
Great West Room, Salon 7

The pull of the earth's gravity on the sea forms the wave, which
is the shape the sea takes as it resists the earth's draw. Rodin
expresses the tension through the personification of earth and sea
in the form of battling spirits.

"It is important to look at the shape from beneath and above, from
high and low, to look down on the contours from above, to see
those which overhang, this is, to become aware of the density of . . .
human (form)." — A. Rodin

68. *Orpheus and the Maenades*   Marble   before 1889
Great West Room, Salon 7

The Maenades were women who worshipped Bacchus. During the Bacchanale, they tore Orpheus to pieces because he took no interest in any woman after Eurydice's death. Here, Rodin depicts the moment before Orpheus is devoured by the frenzied Maenades.

69. *The Thinker* Bronze 1880
A figure with the same dimensions stands in the center of the lintel of
The Gates of Hell. Salon 9

The original *Thinker* is near the top of *The Gates of Hell,* a
Christ-like figure judging the damned. Later, as with many of his
Gates figures, Rodin developed the piece as an independent work.
When first designing *The Gates,* Rodin thought of using Dante,
seated on a rock, creating the plan for his epic work *The Divine
Comedy.* But the image of Dante, thin and ascetic, seemed
inappropriate. The powerful, taut, athletic body of *The Thinker*
lends more power to the image.

"What makes my *Thinker* think, is that he thinks not only with his
brain, with his knitted brow, his distended nostrils, and his
compressed lips, but with every muscle of his arms, back and legs,
with his clenched fists and gripping toes." — A. Rodin

140

70.   *The Thinker*   Salon 9

71. *The Prodigal Son*   Bronze   before 1889   Salon 9

Originally used in *The Gates of Hell, The Prodigal Son* symbolizes
the despair and agony of the damned, evoked by the thrust of his
body as he seems to emit "cries lost in heaven."

72.   *The Prodigal Son*   Salon 9

73. *The Prodigal Son* Salon 9

74. *The Danaïd*   Marble   1885   Salon 10

"Intelligence designs but the heart does the modelling."—A. Rodin

This piece carries the signatures of both Rodin and Jules Desbois (1851-1935), an assistant and sometime collaborator, whose talent was occasionally acknowledged in this manner by Rodin.

76. *She Who Was Once the Helmet-Maker's Beautiful Wife (The Old Courtesan)*
Bronze   1880-1883   Salon 10

For this sculpture, inspired by a François Villon ballad, Rodin used as a model the eighty-year old mother of an Italian artist who had come on foot from her country to see her son before she died. Rodin unhesitatingly represented her sorrow and desperation as well as her physical decrepitude, for all these qualities were beautiful to him.

"When an artist . . . softens the grimace of pain, the shapelessness of age, the hideousness of perversion, when he arranges nature — veiling, disguising, tempering it to please an ignorant public — then he is creating ugliness because he fears the truth. To any artist worthy of the name, all in nature is beautiful because his eyes, fearless and accepting all exterior truth, read then, as in an open book . . . all the inner truth." — A. Rodin

77.   Overview of Salon 10
Fugitive Love   Marble   about 1887   in the foreground

78. *Fugitive Love*   Marble   about 1887   Salon 10

Originally intended for *The Gates of Hell*, this piece suggests the
vain effort of a man trying to grasp a fleeing woman, who, for
Rodin, signified elusive beauty as well as an eternal object of passion.
The sculptor based the piece upon the story of Paolo and Francesca
in Dante's *The Divine Comedy*, whose adulterous love doomed them
to eternal frustration in the second circle of hell. They are caught,
almost touching, almost kissing, but the strong winds prevent their
ever fulfilling their desires. In the context of *The Gates*, the sculpture
represents the punishment for succumbing to the temptation of illicit
carnal pleasure.

79. *Aphrodite*   Plaster   before 1889
A bronze cast stands in the corridor between Salon 10 and Salon 11.   Museum Reserves

"Nature unifies details because she is so simple; she joins all planes,
all contours, in a single unity . . . Simplicity stabilizes theat which
is essential."—A. Rodin

80. *Second Model for the Monument to The Burghers of Calais without a pedastal*
Bronze   1885   Salon 11

Rodin worked hardest on their hands. He shaped all kinds of hands, expressing the gamut of human suffering. Then he attached them to arms that fitted them best and assembled legs and torsos, which he called his giblets.

Originally the monument was supposed to be only of Eustache de Saint-Pierre, but Rodin felt that it was the group's collective bravery that ought to be praised, as well as their individual suffering. They are united by their moment of common destiny, a destiny which each chose freely.

The monument, unveiled on June 3, 1895, was erected neither in the place nor in the manner indicated by Rodin.

"I wanted to have the statues fixed one behind the other in the flags of the square in front of the Town Hall of Calais, like a living rosary of suffering and sacrifice. They would then have looked as if they were setting off from the Town Hall towards the camp of Edward III, and the modern people of Calais, almost rubbing shoulders with them, would have felt more keenly their traditional solidarity with these heroes." —A. Rodin

81. *Nude Study for Eustache de Saint-Pierre, one of The Burghers of Calais*
Bronze   1885   Salon 11

82. *Colossal Head of Jean D'Aire, one of The Burghers of Calais*
Bronze   1886-1889   Salon 11

83.   Overview of Salon 11
Several bronze studies for the monument to *The Burghers of Calais*   1884-1895

84. *Nude Study for Pierre de Wiessant, one of The Burghers of Calais*
Bronze   1885   Salon 11

85.   *Second Model for the Monument to The Burghers of Calais without a pedestal*
Bronze   1885   Salon 11

86. *Second Model for the Monument to The Burghers of Calais without a pedestal* Salon 11

173

87. *The Good Spirit* Bronze about 1900 Salon 12

"I always have living models before my eyes. Not only do I study them when actually working on a sculpture, but I continuously have around me nude models, men and women, walking about in my studio to fill my mind with their forms and movements. Thus the nude, which for my contemporaries is an exceptional vision . . . is as familiar to me as to the ancient Greeks who could contemplate it almost constantly at the palestra. I am careful never to impose an attitude on my models; the very thought of constraining Nature, twisting it to order, is repugnant to me. No, when one of them near me catches my eye, I ask him or her to stay as they are awhile and hasten to make a rough of what I see . . . I am content to let them move about as they please. Any attitude that is imposed is unnatural and useless to study. It is replacing the infinite, interrupting and isolating the secret laws of our being; the body loses its charm and becomes absurd and ridiculous." — A. Rodin

177

89. *Georges Clémenceau* Tinted plaster   1911
Prime Minister of France (1906-1909 and 1917-1919)   Salon 13

Georges Clémenceau, known as "The Tiger," posed for Rodin for
eighteen sittings. When Rodin finally showed him the completed
portrait, Clémenceau complained that Rodin made him look like
an old Chinese maggot, and he insisted that it be called "Portrait of
an Unknown Man" when exhibited at the Salon des Artistes
Français.

90. *Gustav Mahler* Bronze 1909
Austrian Composer. Salon 13

It was actually Mario Meurnier, Rodin's secretary, with a remarkable resemblance to Mahler, who posed for this bust. Rodin often used people who closely resembled his actual subjects as models for his portraits.

91.   Overview of Salon 14
Several bronze studies for the *Monument to Balzac*   1892-1897

92.   *Study for the Monument to Balzac: Balzac Wearing the Robe of a Dominican Friar*
Bronze   1892   Salon 14

In July 1891, the committee of the Société des Gens de Lettres headed by Emile Zola commissioned Rodin to do a statue of Balzac to be completed in eighteen months. Rodin tirelessly researched all aspects of Balzac, including reading his works, travelling to Tours, the province where Balzac was born, and having Balzac's tailor make him a suit of clothes in Balzac's dimensions.

"I think of Balzac's intense labor, of the difficulty of his life, of his incessant battles and of his great courage. I would express all that."—A. Rodin

When finally in 1891 Rodin exhibited the first plaster cast, the public reacted violently. One critic encouraged the public to "take a pick-axe and smash the shameful block to pieces." Another dubbed it, ". . . the mask of a rabid cat. . ." Opponents and supporters of Rodin fought duels over the artistic value of the statue. The controversy took on a political overtone when the press linked the Dreyfusards and Rodin's supporters as being in league with one another to insidiously undermine the moral strength of the French state.

"If truth must die, my Balzac will be smashed to pieces by generations to come . . . but I think that by force or by persuasion, it will find a way into men's minds."—A. Rodin

184

93. *Balzac* *Last Study before the Final Monument* Bronze 1897 Salon 14

94. *Balzac Last Study before the Final Monument* Salon 14

95.   Overview of Salon 14
Study of a Head for the Monument to Balzac   Bronze   1892-1893
in the foreground.   Salon 14

96. Overview of Salon 14
Several bronze studies for the *Monument to Balzac* 1892-1897

97. *Balzac Study for a Bust after a Daguerreotype by Bisson*
Bronze   1892-1893   Salon 14

98. *Balzac Nude Study* Bronze 1892-1893 Salon 14

99. *Balzac Nude Study* Salon 14

100. Overview of Salon 14
Several bronze studies for the *Monument to Balzac* 1892-1897 and for the
Monument to the American Painter, Whistler 1903, never actually cast.

101. *Model for the Monument to Claude Lorraine*   Bronze   1889
Erected in Nancy.   Salon 14

Rodin designed the monument to the seventeenth century landscape
painter Claude Lorraine for the town of Nancy. During the inaugural
ceremony, the statue was protested as "unhealthy." To appease
public criticism, Rodin modified the horses at the base of the statue.
The Apollo group symbolizes poetic and artistic inspiration and
Rodin appropriately placed the image bursting forth from the base
of the piece, analogous to such inspiration bursting forth from the
soul of the artist.

102.   Overview of Salon 14
The Earth   Bronze   1884   in the foreground.

According to Georges Grappe, the late curator of the Rodin
Museum, Rodin always felt uneasy about this work. Indeed in 1913,
Rodin charged an art dealer with falsely selling *The Earth* as
Rodin's, when he never remembered doing it. Later Rodin admitted
making a mistake and that the work was really his. It ranks among
the most daring of Rodin's sculptures in its suggestion of a gigantic
slug of a subhuman species still attached to primeval mud. It evokes
the concept of the earth as the source and destination of all life.

103. *Muse* Bronze 1903 Salon 14
Study for the *Monument to the American Painter, Whistler,* conceived in London, never actually cast.

Alphonse Legros, a schoolmate of Rodin, who lived in England and taught art at the South Kensington school, introduced the sculptor to the English art world, thus helping Rodin to achieve renown on both sides of the English Channel. When the famous American expatriate painter James Whistler died, his friends asked Rodin to prepare a monument to the artist, as well as to succeed Whistler as President of the International Society of Painters, Sculptors, and Engravers.

104.	*Crouching Bather*	Bronze	around 1880	Salon 15

"I have come to realize that geometry is at the bottom sentiment or rather that each expression of sentiment is made by a movement governed by geometry. Geometry is everywhere present in Nature. A woman combing her hair goes through a series of rhythmic movements which constitute a beautiful harmony." — A. Rodin

105. *Pygmalion and Galatea*   Bronze   1889   Salon 16

Here once again Rodin displays his conceptual genius by insisting on pursuing a nontraditional approach to a heretofore sacrosanct subject.

He depicts Pygmalion not as a highly refined sculptor of the golden age of Greece, but more as a primitive, decidely closer to beast than to man. Galatea is shown as shyly twisting her body away from his lusting stare. Her rejection of him is in no sense intellectual but wholly instinctive.

106. *Pygmalion and Galatea*   Salon 16

107. *Andromède* Bronze 1885 Salon 16

"Those who wish to penetrate into some of the invariable rules
Nature follows in composing should observe her opposition of a flat
to a round, the one being the foil of the other. They should also
notice her gradations and contrasts of light producing color into the
real object and should be careful not to produce effects that are out
of accordance with the natural ones." — A. Rodin

108.   *Daphnis and Lycenion*   Bronze   before 1886   Salon 16

The concept for the sculpture was inspired by an ancient Greek romance in which Daphnis, a young woman, learns the art of lovemaking from Lycenion: later, Daphnis imparts her knowledge to Chloë, a simple shepherd, who was much taken with her. Rodin used as his models two female dancers from the Opera whom Degas had recommended to him for his work.

109. *Cupid and Psyche*   Plaster   before 1886   Museum Reserves

Rodin gave a tactile quality to his sculpture, expressing the thrill of an embrace and the excitement of passion.

"The great point is to feel, to live, to hope, and to thrill, to be a man before being an artist. Art is only feeling. But without the knowledge of volumes, proportions, and colors, without manual skill, the most vivid feeling is paralyzed." — A. Rodin

213

110. *Pallas Athena with the Parthenon*   Marble and Plaster   1896
Museum Conservation

The Italian wife of the Australian painter, Russel, posed for the sculpture; Rodin was obviously inspired by the woman's strong classical features.

In placing the Parthenon, the temple of Pallas Athena, goddess of wisdom, on the top of her head like a crown, Rodin refers to the birth of Athena, in which she sprang from Zeus' head, as well as stating his belief that the beauty of ancient Greek culture emananted from the beauty of the Greek mind, for the Parthenon is associated with the seat of that culture.

"The (ancient) Greek women were beautiful, but their beauty lived above all in the minds of the sculptors who carved them . . ." —A. Rodin

111. *The Thinker* The dome of the Invalides 1676 by the architect, Jules Hardouin-Mansart in the background

112. *Eve* Bronze 1881 One of the statues surrounding the basin in the back of the garden of the Rodin Museum.

113. *The facade of the Hôtel Biron bordered by the Courtyard of Honor,*
built between 1728 and 1731 by the architect Jean Aubert, and planned by Jacques
Gabriel. The dome of the Invalides, built by the architect Jules Hardouin-Mansart,
(1676) in the background.

Wherever possible, we have indicated the location of the sculpture in the Rodin Museum at the time the photographs were taken, but occasionally they are moved from one place to another by the Museum administration.